BRUNO MARS

FAMOUS MUSICIAN

KATIE LAJINESS

BIG BUDDY **POP** BIOGRAPHIES

Big Buddy Books
An Imprint of Abdo Publishing
abdopublishing.com

abdopublishing.com

Published by Abdo Publishing, a division of ABDO, PO Box 398166, Minneapolis, Minnesota 55439.
Copyright © 2018 by Abdo Consulting Group, Inc. International copyrights reserved in all countries.
No part of this book may be reproduced in any form without written permission from the publisher.
Big Buddy Books™ is a trademark and logo of Abdo Publishing.

Printed in the United States of America, North Mankato, Minnesota.
092017
012018

THIS BOOK CONTAINS
RECYCLED MATERIALS

Cover Photo: Kevin Winter/Getty Images.
Interior Photos: ASSOCIATED PRESS (pp. 9, 23); Bryan Bedder/Getty Images (p. 21); Dimitrios
    Kambouris/Getty (p. 19); Jamie Squire/Getty Images (p. 27); Jason Merritt/Getty Images
    (p. 11); Joe Scarnici/Getty Images (p. 25); Kevin Winter/Getty Images (p. 13); Kevork Djansezian/
    Getty Images (pp. 15, 29); Larry Busacca/Getty Images (p. 6); Matt Winkelmeyer/Getty Images
    (p. 17); Moses Robinson/Getty Images (p. 5).

Coordinating Series Editor: Tamara L. Britton
Contributing Editor: Jill Roesler
Graphic Design: Jenny Christensen

Publisher's Cataloging-in-Publication Data

Names: Lajiness, Katie, author.
Title: Bruno Mars / by Katie Lajiness.
Description: Minneapolis, Minnesota : Abdo Publishing, 2018. | Series: Big buddy pop biographies |
    Includes online resources and index.
Identifiers: LCCN 2017943938 | ISBN 9781532112171 (lib.bdg.) | ISBN 9781614799245 (ebook)
Subjects: LCSH: Mars, Bruno, (Peter Hernandez), 1985-.--Juvenile literature. | Singers--Juvenile
    literature. | Musicians--Juvenile literature. | United States--Juvenile literature.
Classification: DDC 782.42164092 [B]--dc23
LC record available at https://lccn.loc.gov/2017943938

CONTENTS

HIT SENSATION.................................. 4

SNAPSHOT 5

FAMILY TIES 6

EARLY YEARS 8

BIG BREAK.................................. 10

SUPERSTAR.................................. 14

SCREEN TIME.................................. 18

HIT SONGS.................................. 20

GRAMMY AWARDS.................................. 22

GIVING BACK 24

SUPER BOWL.................................. 26

BUZZ.................................. 28

GLOSSARY 30

ONLINE RESOURCES 31

INDEX 32

HIT SENSATION

Bruno Mars is a talented singer, songwriter, and music **producer**. He is known for writing catchy **pop** music with upbeat **lyrics**. His live **performances** are big and bold!

SNAPSHOT

NAME:
Peter Gene Hernandez

BIRTHDAY:
October 8, 1985

BIRTHPLACE:
Honolulu, Hawaii

POPULAR ALBUMS:
24K Magic, Unorthodox Jukebox, Doo-Wops & Hooligans

FAMILY TIES

Peter Gene Hernandez was born in Honolulu, Hawaii, on October 8, 1985. His parents are Bernadette and Pete Hernandez. He has five **siblings**.

Peter's parents had a band called the Love Notes. His father played **percussion**. His mother was a singer. Sadly, she died in 2013.

Bruno's father is from Puerto Rico. His mother was from the Philippines.

WHERE IN THE WORLD?

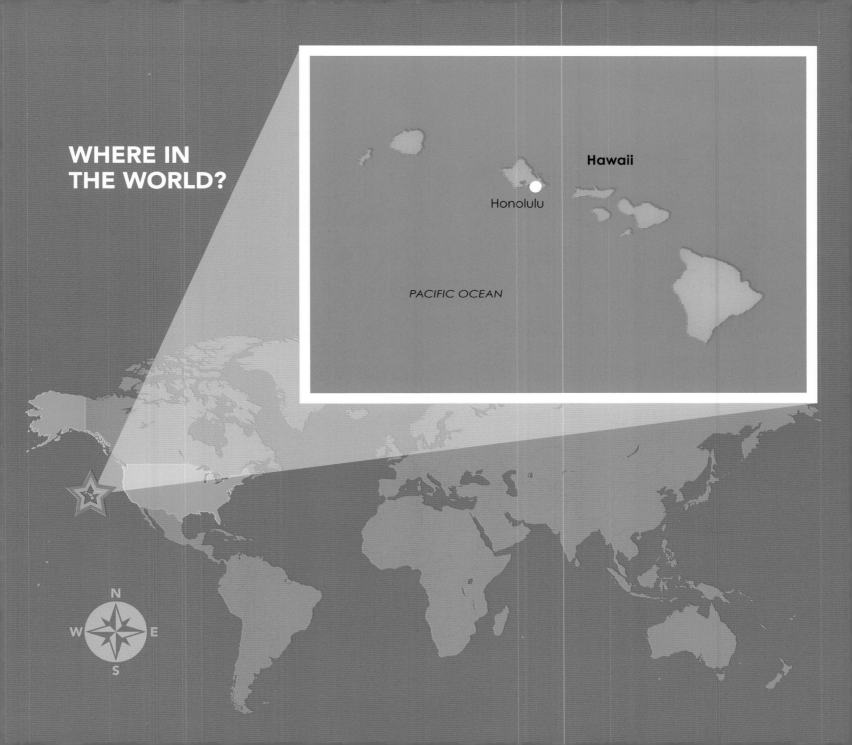

Hawaii

Honolulu

PACIFIC OCEAN

N
W E
S

EARLY YEARS

Early on, Peter loved music. By age four, he began **performing** like singer Elvis Presley. In 1992, Peter did his Elvis **impression** in the movie *Honeymoon in Vegas*.

Peter's dad taught him to play the bongos. Later, Peter learned to play bass, guitar, **percussion**, and piano.

DID YOU KNOW **?**
As a young child, Peter earned the nickname Bruno.

Elvis Presley was a popular American performer from the 1950s to the 1970s. He was known for his flashy outfits and his singing voice.

BIG BREAK

After high school, Peter moved to Los Angeles, California. During this time, he began **performing** under the name Bruno Mars.

In 2004, Bruno signed with Motown Records. He then began working with a group of songwriters called the Smeezingtons. Together, they wrote and **produced** many songs.

In 2009, Bruno cowrote "Nothin' on You" with the Smeezingtons (*shown*) and hip-hop artist B.o.B. Soon after, Bruno signed with the record label Elektra.

As Bruno's fame grew, he wanted to make his own music. He **released** a four-song **EP** in 2010 called *It's Better If You Don't Understand*.

Later that year, Bruno released his first album, *Doo-Wops & Hooligans*. It included hits "Just the Way You Are," "Grenade," and "The Lazy Song."

DID YOU KNOW?
Bruno was one of *Time* magazine's 100 Most Influential People in 2011.

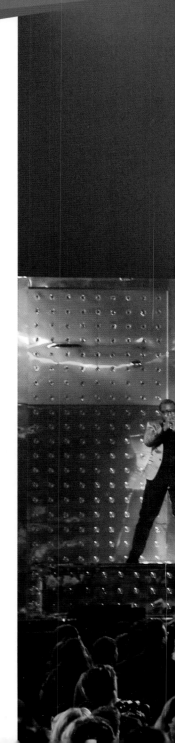

At the 2012 Grammy Awards, Bruno sang his hit song "Runaway Baby."

SUPERSTAR

In 2012, Bruno continued his success with his second album, *Unorthodox Jukebox*. The album included "Locked Out of Heaven," "When I Was Your Man," and "Treasure."

Bruno's biggest hit yet was the 2014 single "Uptown Funk." He and **producer** Mark Ronson cowrote the song.

DID YOU KNOW?
The single "Uptown Funk" has sold more copies than Bruno's three albums combined!

Bruno, Mark Ronson (*right*), and their team won a 2015 MTV Video Music Award for "Uptown Funk."

Bruno held onto his superstar status when he **released** another hit album after four years. He surprised his fans with a new single, "24K Magic," a new album cover, and a music video. His third album, *24K Magic*, has sold 1 million copies.

DID YOU KNOW
As of 2017, Bruno had nearly 30 million followers on Twitter.

In 2016, Bruno went to the iHeartRadio Theater in Los Angeles. There, he let fans listen to a preview of *24K Magic*.

SCREEN TIME

Bruno acted charming and funny on TV. He has been on *The Ellen DeGeneres Show* several times. Once, Bruno sang with a six-year-old fan named Kai.

In 2016, he appeared on *The Late Late Show with James Corden*. Bruno and James had fun singing **pop** songs while driving in a car.

DID YOU KNOW?
Bruno was the voice of Roberto in *Rio 2*.

Bruno has performed on TV for events such as fashion shows.

HIT SONGS

Bruno has written many hit songs. He has even written songs for other **pop** stars to sing. Bruno and Adele wrote "All I Ask" together.

Many of Bruno's number-one songs have stayed on the music charts for several weeks. In 2010, "Just the Way You Are" was a top song for 48 weeks.

In 2013, "When I Was Your Man" topped the charts for 35 weeks.

GRAMMY AWARDS

Over the years, Bruno has accepted many music **awards**. In 2013, *Unorthodox Jukebox* earned a **Grammy Award** for Best **Pop** Vocal Album.

As of 2017, Bruno had won all four Grammys for which he had been **nominated**. Winning a Grammy is one of the biggest accomplishments in the music business.

"Uptown Funk" was a worldwide hit. It won the 2016 Grammy for Record of the Year.

GIVING BACK

Giving back has been very important to Bruno. He has worked with **charities** that use music to help those in need. Bruno has supported groups such as the GRAMMY Foundation, MusiCares, and **Musicians** on Call.

Bruno sang at a 2013 charity event for the EIF Cancer Research Fund.

SUPER BOWL

The Super Bowl is the largest football game of the year. The **performers** are an important part of the Super Bowl Halftime Show.

Bruno has performed in two Super Bowl Halftime Shows. In 2014, he sang many of his popular songs. Two years later, Bruno sang "Uptown Funk" with Beyoncé and the band Coldplay.

DID YOU KNOW?

Bruno is one of six singers who have performed at multiple Super Bowls.

In 2014, more than 115 million people watched Bruno Mars perform in the Super Bowl Halftime Show.

BUZZ

In March 2017, Bruno received the iHeartRadio Innovator **Award**. It honors some of the best-selling artists of all time.

Later in 2017, Bruno began an 85-city tour in Belgium. From July to November, he traveled around the United States for the tour. Fans are excited to see what Bruno will do next!

Bruno performed a tribute to the late singer Prince. Bruno is dressed in one of Prince's most famous styles.

GLOSSARY

award something that is given in recognition of good work or a good act.

charity a group or a fund that helps people in need.

EP extended play. A music recording with more than one song, but fewer than a full album.

Grammy Award any of the awards given each year by the National Academy of Recording Arts and Sciences. Grammy Awards honor the year's best accomplishments in music.

impression an imitation of a famous person done for entertainment.

lyrics the words to a song.

musician someone who writes, sings, or plays music.

nominate to name as a possible winner.

percussion the beating or striking of a musical instrument.

perform to do something in front of an audience. A performance is the act of doing something, such as singing or acting, in front of an audience. A performer is the person who gives the performance.

pop relating to popular music.

producer a person who oversees the making of a movie, a play, an album, or a radio or television show. To produce is to oversee the making of a movie, an album, or a radio or television show.

release to make available to the public.

sibling a brother or a sister.

ONLINE RESOURCES

Booklinks
NONFICTION NETWORK
FREE! ONLINE NONFICTION RESOURCES

To learn more about Bruno Mars, visit **abdobooklinks.com**.
These links are routinely monitored and updated to provide
the most current information available.

INDEX

Adele **20**

awards **13, 15, 22, 23, 28**

Belgium **28**

Beyoncé **26**

B.o.B **11**

California **10, 17**

charities **24, 25**

Coldplay (band) **26**

Corden, James **18**

Doo-Wops & Hooligans (album) **5, 12**

Elektra **11**

Ellen DeGeneres Show, The (television show) **18**

family **6, 8**

Hawaii **5, 6**

Honeymoon in Vegas (movie) **8**

iHeartRadio Theater **17**

It's Better If You Don't Understand (EP) **12**

Kai **18**

Late Late Show with James Corden, The (television show) **18**

Love Notes, the (band) **6**

Motown Records **10**

music charts **20, 21**

music tour **28**

Philippines **6**

Presley, Elvis **8, 9**

Prince **29**

Puerto Rico **6**

Rio 2 (movie) **18**

Ronson, Mark **14, 15**

Smeezingtons, the **10, 11**

social media **16**

Super Bowl, the **26, 27**

Time (magazine) **12**

24K Magic (album) **5, 16, 17**

United States **28**

Unorthodox Jukebox (album) **5, 14, 22**